The big book of practical jokes
100 ways to fool your friends!

Gyles Brandreth

illustrated by Jacqui Sinclair

CAROUSEL BOOKS
A DIVISION OF TRANSWORLD PUBLISHERS LTD.

other books by GYLES BRANDRETH

DOMINO GAMES AND PUZZLES
NUMBER GAMES AND PUZZLES
GAMES AND PUZZLES WITH COINS AND MATCHES
PENCIL AND PAPER GAMES AND PUZZLES
HOTCHPOTCH
THE ROYAL QUIZ BOOK
BRAIN TEASERS AND MIND-BENDERS
EDWARD LEAR'S BOOK OF MAZES
BIG BOOK OF SECRETS
PUZZLE PARTY FUN BOOK
THE DAFT DICTIONARY
JOKES, JOKES, JOKES: A JOKE FOR EVERY DAY OF THE YEAR
THE GREAT BIG FUNNY BOOK
PROJECT: THE HUMAN BODY
PROJECT: NUMBER FUN

All published by CAROUSEL BOOKS.

CONTENTS

COMPETITION

Gyles Brandreth and his publishers are looking for lots more practical jokes to include in the SECOND BIG BOOK OF PRACTICAL JOKES. If you have any ideas for original practical jokes, why not send them to us? There is a first prize of £500 for the best practical joke submitted. Full details of how to enter this exciting competition can be found on page 129.

WARNING

When planning a practical joke choose your victim with care. Make sure it's someone with a sense of humour.

Most of the jokes in this book you could try on anyone, anywhere, at any time — but when you see the skull and crossbones watch out. It's a sign that the joke is either rather a messy one — so make sure you try it out of doors on someone who isn't wearing their best clothes — or one that could frighten or upset your victim, especially if they happened to be an elderly or frail person.

PRACTICAL JOKES TO AVOID

1. Any joke where anyone gets hurt.
2. Any joke that ruins the sitting room carpet.
3. Any joke that spoils somebody's birthday.
4. Any joke that makes somebody cry.
5. Any joke that makes somebody blush.
6. Any joke that results in more than £50,000 of damage to property.
7. Any joke that causes loss of life or limb.
8. Any joke that causes 10,000 people to run screaming out of a football stadium.
9. Any joke that results in a world war.
10. Any joke that isn't funny.

PRACTICAL JOKES
NOT
TO AVOID

1 HEAD FIRST

Here's the most famous practical joke of them all. You balance something on top of a door that is slightly ajar, so that when your victim comes into the room and pushes the door open they get hit on the head and you fall about laughing!

But if you try this one you've got to be very, very careful. You can't balance a bucket of water on top of the door, for a start. That would be far too dangerous. Anything that's at all heavy would be dangerous as well. The best thing to use is a **pillow.**

Have fun — but don't be surprised if your victim isn't as amused by the joke as you are!

Take your parents' newspaper and glue the centre pages together!

If you think that might make them CROSS, don't do it! Instead, keep an old copy of the newspaper that your parents have read and secretly swap all the inside pages from the old newspaper with all the inside pages from the new newspaper. If they haven't read the new newspaper, they won't understand when they open it up why it seems to be full of last week's news!

NOW ALL YOU HAVE TO DO IS FILL A TUMBLER WITH WATER AND HOLD IT OVER YOUR HEAD FOR FIVE MINUTES — YOU'RE STAYING UNDER WATER FOR FIVE MINUTES JUST AS YOU PROMISED YOU WOULD!

YOU: Now I want you to add these up:

> One ton of sawdust.
> One ton of chewing gum.
> One ton of marshmallow.
> One ton of bone.
> One ton of fat.

Have you got all that in your head?

VICTIM: Yes.

YOU: I thought so.

THREAD BARE

For this joke you will need:

> **A JACKET**
> **A REEL OF COTTON**
> **A NEEDLE**

To prepare the joke, thread the needle with the cotton and then thread the cotton through the jacket so that just a centimetre or two of cotton shows on the outside of the jacket's shoulder.

Remove the needle and put it away. Put the rest of the reel of cotton in an inside pocket of the jacket. Now put on the jacket and wear it all day.

Sooner or later a victim will come along — probably your mother or somebody else's mother — who will see the little bit of cotton on your shoulder and will try to remove it for you. As soon as they pick up the loose end of cotton, walk away at a brisk pace. Your poor victim will be left holding a length of cotton that gets longer and longer and **longer** and **LONGER!**

7 WATER TORTURE

YOU: Mum, I've run you
a nice hot bath.

MUM: Oh, thank you, dear.
That was very thoughtful.

(MUM goes into the bathroom.
Gets into the bath.)

TEE·HEE

MUM: Aaaaaaaaaaaaarrrrrrgggggghhhhhhhhh!

(Tee-hee! You filled the bath with COLD
water!!)

(**SERIOUS NOTE:** Never play this practical
joke on anyone using **HOT** water.
It could be dangerous.)

8

YOU: I knew an amazing
fellow who had snoo
in his blood.

VICTIM: What's snoo?

YOU: Nothing much.
What's new with you?

9

YOU: I bet you I can kiss this
book inside and
outside without opening it.

VICTIM: I bet you can't.

YOU: I bet you £100 I can.

VICTIM: Okay, you're on.

NOW ALL YOU HAVE TO DO IS KISS THE BOOK ON THE OUTSIDE AND THEN TAKE IT OUT OF DOORS AND KISS IT AGAIN. YOU'VE KISSED THE BOOK INSIDE AND OUTSIDE AND YOU HAVEN'T OPENED IT! WHAT'S MORE, YOU'RE A HUNDRED POUNDS RICHER!

10

To fool the whole family, change the time of day. Make it seem like six o'clock in the evening instead of four in the afternoon.

All you have to do is change every clock and watch in the house and wait to see what happens. Whatever you do, don't keep asking people the time every two minutes or they'll guess something's going on. Just wait for them to look at the kitchen clock and be surprised. If someone says 'The clocks around here are on the blink,' then you can offer to telephone the Speaking Clock. Dial the number for the Speaking Clock, but don't tell anyone what you're really hearing. Tell them that the Speaking Clock says whatever time it is you've changed all the other clocks and watches to!

This is a practical joke that can sometimes back-fire. You might find yourself being sent to bed at five o'clock because your parents thought it was already nine!

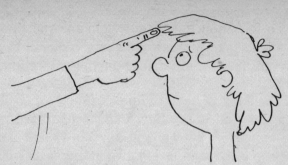

If I lived up here.

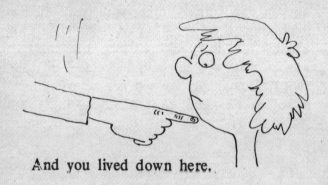

And you lived down here.

Would you come up and see me sometime?

YOU: Here's a pencil and a piece of paper. Now for 10p I'd like you to write a small letter I with a dot over it.

VICTIM: That's easy.

THE VICTIM THEN WRITES:

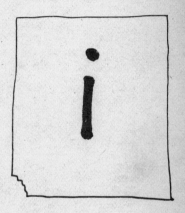

YOU: Wrong! This is a small letter I with a dot over it:

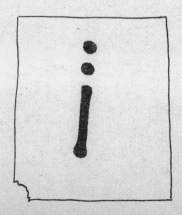

For this joke you need some paper cups and a pin. To prepare for the joke, take all the cups except one of them and prick a few tiny holes around the sides and on the bottom of them. That's all you have to do.

Now when anyone comes to see you and you feel like having some fun, offer them a glass of orange squash. Pour the squash into one of the special cups and give it to them. Every time they take a sip they'll find they're dribbling orange squash all over the place!

You'll never dribble, of course, because you'll make sure you always use the one paper cup that doesn't have any holes in it.

YOU: I bet you can't button up your coat in less than a minute.

VICTIM: I bet you I can.

YOU: I bet you you can't.

VICTIM: Let me try.

YOU: Okay. You've got sixty seconds to button up your coat starting **NOW!**

THE VICTIM STARTS BUTTONING AWAY FURIOUSLY AND AFTER ABOUT TWENTY SECONDS SHOUTS, 'I'VE DONE IT!'

YOU: No, you haven't. I said I bet you couldn't button **up** your coat in less than a minute. You started with the top button and buttoned **down** your coat!

(DON'T WORRY. YOU WON'T LOSE THIS BET.

PEOPLE ALMOST ALWAYS START BUTTONING A COAT FROM THE TOP AND WORK THEIR WAY DOWN.)

If you want to fool a stranger this is a very clever way to do it. It's a joke that works especially well on a train or a bus or in a doctor's waiting room — anywhere, in fact, where lots of people are sitting together who don't really know one another and don't have anything much to do.

What you can do with these people, believe it or not, is make them **yawn.** You don't have to say anything. You don't have to move. All you have to do is yawn yourself. Don't do it too obviously and don't do it too often. Just yawn gently once or twice and watch what happens. Before you can say 'Forty winks' you'll find everyone near you is yawning too. **You** know why they're yawning — but, poor fools, they don't.

18

YOU: How do you spell the word joke?

VICTIM: J, O, K, E.

YOU: How do you spell the word folk?

VICTIM: F, O, L, K.

YOU: How do you spell the word poke?

VICTIM: P, O, K, E.

YOU: How do you spell the white of an egg?

VICTIM: Y, O, L, K.

YOU: That's the yellow of an egg!
The white of an egg is
ALBUMEN!!!

YOU: I bet you can't put your **RIGHT HAND** where your **LEFT HAND** can't reach it.

YOUR VICTIM TRIES AND TRIES AND TRIES AND TRIES — AND FAILS. THEN YOU SHOW HIM HOW IT'S DONE. PLACE YOUR LEFT HAND UNDER YOUR RIGHT ELBOW. NOW YOUR RIGHT HAND CAN'T REACH IT. (YES, IT IS EASY ONCE YOU KNOW HOW, BUT WHEN YOU DON'T KNOW THE SECRET IT SEEMS IMPOSSIBLE.)

20

YOU: If you were walking in a country lane
— and there were no trees to climb
and no holes to hide in
and you didn't have a gun
and there was no one about to
help you — and you saw a grizzly
bear coming towards you,
what would you do?

VICTIM: Run.

YOU: With a bear behind?!

HAVE YOU NOTICED?

Take a piece of paper about ten centimetres square and write a message on it. Fix a little bit of sticky tape to the top of the paper. Now try to stick your notice on to your victim's back without him noticing. The best way is to go up to him from behind and slap him on the back as if you were greeting him in a friendly way. As you slap him on the back you fix the notice firmly on to him. Then you sit back and watch him as he spends the rest of the day wondering why people are laughing behind his back!

If you want to make your joke really **practical,** you can put a special message on his back so that the people who read it will have to do something unusual.

Your victim will wonder why he's so popular!

22 HANDS UP!

If you want to show a friend that not only can you fool him, you also have power over him and can make him do things that you want him to do even if he doesn't want to do them himself, here's how.

Get your victim to stand in a doorway and to push the **backs** of his hands against the door frame as hard as he possibly can. He must keep pushing for at least a minute. (Yes, a minute is a long time — especially when you're standing in a doorway pushing the backs of your hands against the doorframe, but if he does it for anything less than sixty seconds the trick won't work.)

When the time's up, tell him to relax his arms and move away from the door. As he does so, say 'Stick 'em up!' and whether he likes it or not, both his arms will automatically rise up in the air!!

Put a little of your mother's
lipstick or eyeshadow on to
your first finger and forefinger.

Then tell a friend to stand still. Tell him
he's got a smudge on his nose. (He hasn't, of
course.) As you pretend to wipe the smudge
away that isn't there, you actually put a
smudge on to his nose!

And if you want people to think you've
got the measles or the chicken pox — or the
Dreaded Spotted Fever — put small spots of
lipstick all over your face and arms and
hands.

24

I bet I can jump across the street.

I bet you can't.

I bet you £100 I can.

I bet you £100 you can't

O.K. Watch.

(You now walk across the street and jump!)

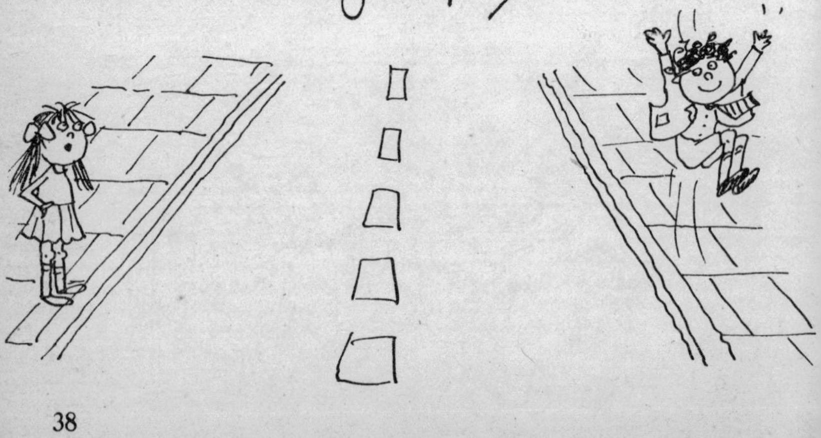

YOU: I'm going to ask you three questions. And to each of the three questions you can either answer **YES** or **NO** — but you mustn't speak. You can only give me your answer with your fingers.

Here's how. Make a circle with the thumb and the little finger of your right hand, pressing the nail of your little finger into the underside of the thumb, like this:

Now hold your other three fingers together and press them down flat on to the edge of a table, like this.

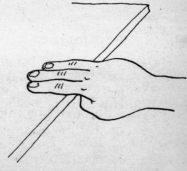

To answer Question Number One you must use the finger next to your thumb. To answer Question Number Two you must use your index finger. To answer Question Number Three you must use your third finger:

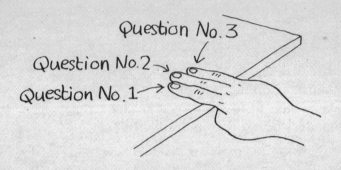

If you want to answer **YES**, just wiggle the finger in question. To answer **NO**, lift the finger three centimetres away from the table. When answering a question, you must **not** move any of your other fingers or your thumb.

If you're ready, I'll ask the three questions.

Number One. Are you feeling happy today? (The victim can answer either YES or NO by wiggling his first finger or by lifting it three centimetres off the table.)

Number Two. Is your birthday this month? (The victim can answer either YES or NO by wiggling his index finger or by lifting it three centimetres off the table.)

Number Three. Are you a stinking, blinking idiot? (The poor victim can only answer YES because he'll find that he can wiggle his third finger but he simply can't lift it three centimetres off the table without moving his other fingers!)

YOU: What does it say here?

A FOOL
IN THE
THE FAMILY

VICTIM: A FOOL IN THE FAMILY.

YOU: Wrong!

(Did you think it said **A FOOL IN THE FAMILY** too? Look again carefully. It says **A FOOL IN THE THE FAMILY!**)

27 JAM PACKED HANDSHAKE

YOU: Hello.

VICTIM: Hello.

YOU SHAKE HANDS.

VICTIM: Uuuuuuuuuugggggghhhh!

YOU: Sorry I can't stay!

All you did was shake hands with an old friend — he just didn't expect you to have a spoonful of strawberry jam in the palm of your right hand.

YOU: Ask me if I'm
a double-decker bus.

VICTIM: Are you a double-decker bus?

YOU: Yes. Now ask me if I'm
a bicycle.

VICTIM: Are you a bicycle?

YOU: Of course not, stupid! I just told
you I'm a double-decker bus.

YOU: I bet you I can put this tenpenny piece somewhere where **EVERYBODY** can see it, except for you.

VICTIM: I bet you can't.

YOU: I bet you the 10p I can.

VICTIM: Okay.

NOW ALL YOU DO IS PLACE THE 10p COIN ON TOP OF YOUR VICTIM'S HEAD. HE CAN'T SEE IT THERE — BUT EVERYBODY ELSE CAN!

For this joke you need talcum powder — or baby powder — and a victim who wears a hat.

All you do is sprinkle a good bit of powder inside the hat and lie in wait. When your victim comes along and puts on her hat, her head and hair will get covered in the powder!

(**DON'T** do this with flour. It's much too difficult to wash out of your hair.)

YOU: I bet you I can push myself through that keyhole.

VICTIM: I bet you you can't.

YOU: I bet you £100 I can.

VICTIM: Okay, you're on.

NOW WRITE THE WORD 'MYSELF' ON A TINY PIECE OF PAPER AND PUSH THE PAPER THROUGH THE KEYHOLE. YOU'VE PUSHED 'MYSELF' THROUGH THE KEYHOLE, JUST AS YOU SAID YOU WOULD!

33

CHEERS!

If there is someone in your family who likes to drink spirits like **GIN** or **VODKA** or who likes to drink **RED WINE,** you can play a good practical joke on them.

GIN or VODKA

You have to plan ahead with this joke. Collect and keep an old gin or vodka bottle once it's empty. Fill this old bottle with cold **water.** Put the old bottle filled with water in the place of a new bottle filled with gin or vodka. Hide the new bottle and watch what happens when your victim pours himself a glass of gin or vodka and tries to drink it!

RED WINE

You can do exactly the same with an empty bottle of red wine. Instead of filling it up with water, though, you must fill it up with blackcurrant juice.

35 STRINGS ATTACHED

Tie a cup to a door knob exactly like this:

Now hand your victim a pair of scissors and challenge him to cut the string **without** letting the cup fall to the ground and **without** touching the cup. Bet him £100 he can't do it.

Your victim will give up pretty quickly. When he does, all you have to do is cut through one of the loops of the bow, and you've done what you bet him he couldn't do — cut the string without touching the cup and without letting it fall to the ground.

You can have great fun with a balloon. Blow it up, but don't tie up. Instead, let the air out of it very slowly pulling the neck as you do so.

You'll find the air leaving the balloon makes some **very** funny noises. Experiment with different ways of letting the air out — sometimes do it quickly, sometimes slowly, sometimes hold the neck tightly, sometimes hardly hold it at all — and you'll find the noises change.

If nobody knows you've got a blown up balloon behind your back, they will certainly be fooled by the amazing noises it makes as you let it down!

(DON'T TRY DOING THIS AT SCHOOL — EXCEPT PERHAPS ON THE LAST DAY OF TERM!)

YOU: **ANTIDISESTABLISH-MENTARIANISM**
is one of the longest words in the dictionary. How many Ts are there in that?

VICTIM: Three or four?

YOU: No, just two.
T, h, a, T!

This is a classic April Fool. It never fails.

To do it properly you need a very long tape measure, the sort that builders and surveyors use. (The games teacher at school might have one for measuring playing areas and running tracks.) If you can't get hold of a long tape measure, a length of string that runs to at least 10 metres will do instead.

Take your tape measure or your string out into the street and ask a passer-by if they will help you measure a nearby building.

Hand your victim one end of the tape or string and then walk round the building, leaving him where he is and unravelling the tape or string as you go.

When you get round the corner of the building find another and ask him if he will help you. Give him the other end of the tape or string!

Now disappear to a spot where you can watch your victims but they can't see you. Eventually, they'll start to wonder what's going on and they'll go round the bend to find out!

YOU: There was a delicious cream cake here a minute ago. Who's taken it? Did you steal it?

VICTIM: No, of course not.

YOU: Oh, well, never mind. Let's play a game.

VICTIM: Okay.

YOU: I'll start by saying 'I one it', then you say 'I two it', then I'll say 'I three it' and so on. Okay?

VICTIM: Okay.

YOU: I one it.

VICTIM: I two it.

YOU: I three it.

VICTIM: I four it.

YOU: I five it.

VICTIM: I six it.

YOU: I seven it.

VICTIM: I eight it.

YOU: I thought you had, you greedy pig!

40 PRESENT LAUGHTER

Give your victim an enormous box beautifully wrapped.

Inside the box is a parcel carefully wrapped.

Inside the first layer of wrapping there's another layer.

Inside the second layer there's a third layer.

Inside the third there's a fourth. And so on and so on.

Make sure there are at least **TEN** layers of wrapping — leading to an old potato!

YOU: Here's a marvellous book called **JOKES! JOKES! JOKES!** by Gyles Brandreth. It's a great book — an amazing book. It's so amazing, in fact, that I bet I can put this book somewhere on the floor in this room and you won't be able to jump over it!

VICTIM: Okay, try me.

NOW PUT THE BOOK IN A CORNER OF THE ROOM!

42 APPLE PIE BED

Do you know how to make an apple pie bed? It's easy — and one of the really great practical jokes.

Here is what you do:

1. Take all the sheets and blankets off your victim's bed.

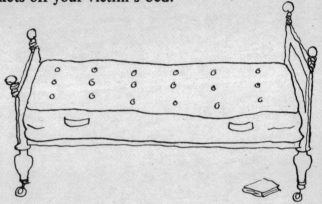

2. Put on the bottom sheet, but only tuck it in at the top.

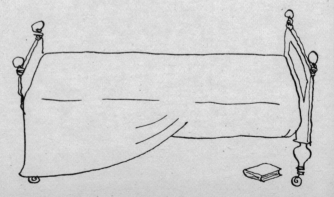

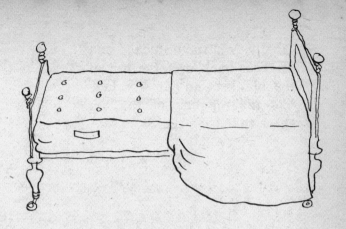

3. Fold the end of the bottom sheet back up so that it hangs loosely over the top half you've already tucked in.

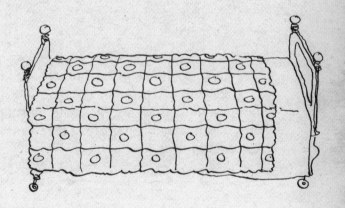

4. Don't bother about a second sheet. You don't need one. Now put on the blankets as usual.

5. Finally, fold the untucked end of sheet back over the top of the blankets and it will **look** like the top end of the top sheet that isn't there!

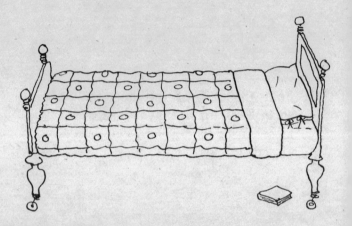

Now the bed looks quite normal. When your victim arrives and jumps into it, though, he'll find it's far from normal. He will only be able to put his feet down a few centimetres!

YOU: I bet you can't stick your tongue out and touch your nose.

YOUR VICTIM TRIES AND TRIES AND TRIES AND TRIES — AND FAILS!

VICTIM: It can't be done.

YOU: Yes it can. Watch.

YOU STICK YOUR TONGUE OUT AND TOUCH YOUR NOSE WITH YOUR FINGER!

YOU: Many years ago in the ancient Kingdom of Siam there was a secret society that only the cleverest and richest people in the country could belong to.

VICTIM: Really?

YOU: The society still exists, but now that Siam has changed its name to Thailand the society is more secret than it's ever been. I'm a member of the society, of course.

VICTIM: Really?

YOU: I'll let you join if you like.

VICTIM: What do I have to do?

YOU: It's very simple. Just close your eyes and spin round five times. Then repeat the ancient oath of the Kingdom of Siam five times. It's in Siamese:

OOO WATA NA SIAM!

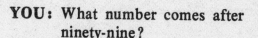

YOU: What number comes after ninety-nine?

VICTIM: One hundred.

YOU: What number comes after nine hundred and ninety-nine?

VICTIM: One thousand.

YOU: What number comes after nine thousand and ninety-nine?

VICTIM: Ten thousand.

YOU: Wrong! Nine thousand one hundred comes after nine thousand and ninety nine. Ten thousand comes after nine thousand nine hundred and ninety nine!

TO MAKE SURE YOU FOOL YOUR VICTIM EVERY TIME WITH THIS TRICK DO IT AS QUICKLY AS POSSIBLE. DON'T GIVE HIM TIME TO THINK OF THE RIGHT ANSWER!

Offer to cook the family breakfast and tell them they needn't worry because you're only going to do something easy like boiled eggs.

When everyone comes into the kitchen to have their eggs you've already started yours and it looks **delicious.** But when they crack into theirs, they're in for a big surprise — because all they've got are empty egg-shells!

When the family **last** had boiled eggs you carefully collected all the empty eggshells at the end of the meal and kept them in a secret place. Having washed and dried the empty egg shells all you had to do to fool everyone was place the empty shells upside down in the egg cups.

WATCH OUT! THERE'S A HENWEIGH ABOUT TO LAND ON YOU.
WHAT'S A HENWEIGH?
OH, ABOUT FOUR POUNDS.

YOU: I'd like to test your eyesight, if you don't mind.

VICTIM: Not at all. Go right ahead.

YOU: Thank you. If you could help me by pointing a finger at your eyes at the side of your head.

VICTIM: Like this?

YOU: That's right. Now please tell me what you can see on my Eye Chart. There are four letters and a drawing. I'd like you to read out the four letters and tell what the drawing is.

VICTIM: I B M T ear.

YOU: Well, you said it!

VOICES FROM NOWHERE

If you want to fool your friends and frighten them, go into a room that's empty and hide in a cupboard or behind the curtains. Make sure it's a room that someone is going to come into — or you'll be all alone in there all day! When someone **does** come into the room, stay hidden and wait for a few minutes before making a sound. Then, all of a sudden, let out a piercing scream! It'll TERRIFY them!

50 CACTUS CAPER

If you want to give your teacher a special present on 1st April, how about this?

On 31st March, tell your teacher that your father has a new hobby. He collects cacti and succulents. Explain to your teacher that your father has recently grown a remarkable new specimen and that you will bring it in tomorrow as a special present for your teacher.

Next day arrive with your present. In fact, it's a scouring pad planted in a small pot of real earth. Unless your teacher knows a lot about cacti and succulents, you could fool him!

YOU: Once upon a time, what animal had six legs and jumped over the moon?

VICTIM: I don't know.

YOU: A cow.

VICTIM: A cow?

YOU: Yes. I added two legs to make it a bit harder.

In secret, you can slice bananas and cut apples in half **INSIDE THEIR SKINS.** The fruit will look perfectly ordinary on the outside, but when any of your victims pick a piece of it up to eat they'll be in for some surprises!

First, here's how to slice your banana.

Take a needle and push it into the banana along the length of one of the seams, like this:

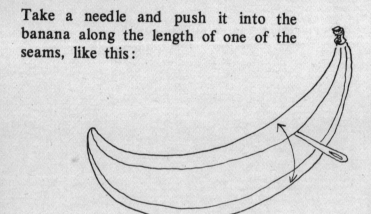

Now move it from side to side. The needle will be cutting the banana inside the skin. Put the needle in at several points up and down the length of the banana and you can slice it into a number of pieces.

When your victim peels the banana, he'll be amazed that the banana inside just falls to pieces!

Cutting an apple in half on the inside isn't so easy. To do this you need a needle and thread. Begin by threading the needle, then pass the needle through the apple from one side to the other, going as close to the apple's skin as you can, like this:

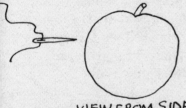

VIEW FROM SIDE

VIEW FROM ABOVE

Then push the needle through the apple again, like this:

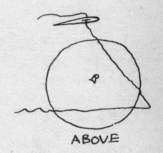

ABOVE

Finally push the needle and thread through the apple for the last time, like this:

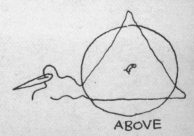

ABOVE

All you now have to do is gently tug at the two ends of the thread. Gradually the thread will cut through the centre of the apple — so that when anyone picks up the apple and starts to peel it they'll be amazed to find it falls apart.

If you want to show off to your friends rather than fool them, you can boast that you're able to break an apple neatly in two with one blow. They won't know that the apple has been specially prepared and they will be most impressed by your strength and skill as the master of fruity Kung Fu.

If you are any good at forging letters you can have a lot of fun. For example, you can forge a letter to your parents telling them they've won £500,000 on the football pools! Or you can forge a letter from your headmaster telling your parents that you have been expelled! Or you can forge a letter to a friend telling him he's going to be made a knight!

You'll find it a lot easier to write forged letters if you can borrow a typewriter. A typed letter always looks that bit more official. And if you really want to do the job properly, you'll send your letter through the post. It's an expensive practical joke, if you count the cost of the stamp, but well worth it!

YOU must show your victim the palm of your right hand. Explain to him that the centre of the palm is where a brand-new baby is sleeping. Show him the exact spot where the baby is. Explain to him that because the baby is so new and tiny everyone has got to be extra specially careful with him. Then say, touching the centre of your palm each time:

Daddy says, 'Don't touch the baby!'
Mummy says, 'Don't touch the baby!'
Brother says, 'Don't touch the baby!'
Sister says, 'Don't touch the baby!'
Grandpa says, 'Don't touch the baby!'
Grandma says, 'Don't touch the baby!'

Now ask the victim: Where is the baby?

When he points to the centre of your palm, smack his hand and shout: **DON'T TOUCH THE BABY!**

If you want to fool your friends and impress them, tell them you're a trained ventriloquist. They won't believe you, but you can prove it.

Get a puppet — or a soft toy — or a pet — or even a real ventriloquist's dummy, if you want to do the job thoroughly — and make them talk. Your friends will be amazed as your dummy speaks but you don't move your lips!

How do you do it? The secret is an **ACCOMPLICE.** Hidden behind a door, or in a cupboard, or behind the curtains, you have another friend and he is your dummy's voice!

56 BATH TIME

This is a good one for 1st April. Wait until either your Mum or your Dad has got into the bath, then go outside the front door and ring the doorbell. Come back in again and rush to the bathroom door.

YOU: Dad! Mum! Come quickly, there's a policeman here to see you.

Seconds later your soaking parent will come out of the bathroom dripping with water and wrapped in wet towels.

YOU: APRIL FOOL!!!

57

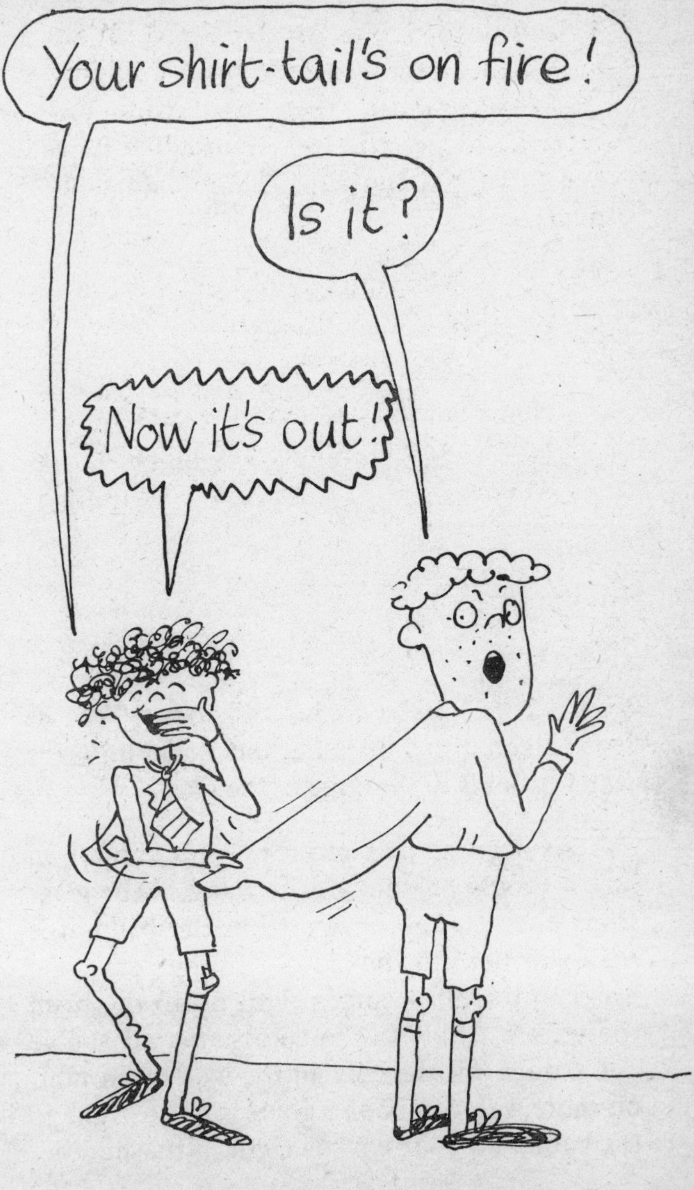

YOU: Here is a glass of water and here is a cork.

Now I bet you can't get the cork to float in the middle of the glass of water.

Your victim tries and tries and tries — but he fails. Each time he puts the cork into the water it floats to the edge of the glass.

As soon as he's given in, you show him how it should be done. If the water in the glass stops about a centimetre from the brim, the cork will float to the side of the glass. If the water in the glass comes right up to the brim the cork will stay in the centre. So all you've got to do is put the cork in the water and pour on more water until the glass is filled right to the brim and your cork is right in the middle.

On a very crowded bus or a very crowded train where you are with a friend but both of you are having to stand up because the bus or train is so full of people, suddenly turn to your friend and say, **'DON'T LOOK NOW, BUT BEFORE YOU LEFT HOME YOU FORGOT TO PUT YOUR SKIRT/TROUSERS ON!'**

EEK

YOU: Do you collect
stamps?

VICTIM: Yes.

YOU: Good. Here's one for your
collection. (And as you say
it you stamp on the
victim's foot!)

**DON'T WORRY IF THE VICTIM SAYS HE
DOESN'T COLLECT STAMPS. THERE
ARE TWO EQUALLY GOOD VERSIONS
OF THE SAME TRICK.**

YOU: Do you collect
stamps?

VICTIM: No.

YOU: Well, you ought to. It's
great fun. Here's one to
start you off with!

61 LET RIP!

Put a fifty penny piece on the ground and stand near it. Position yourself so you are near enough to the coin to make sure no one walks off with it, but try not to look as if you have noticed that the coin is there.

When someone comes along and bends down to pick up the coin, tear a sheet of paper behind your back. Whoever's bending over will think they've torn their trousers!

(Some types of paper make better ripping sounds than others. Experiment with different pieces of paper to see which one you think sounds most realistic.)

Ask a friend if they could do you a big favour. When they say Yes, tell them you'd like them to pop into the local supermarket and get a few things for you. Give them a £1 note and tell them that if they manage to get everything on the shopping list they can keep the change. Give them the £1 and the shopping list — but make sure the list is folded in two so they don't look at it at once.

1 pkt. hot ice cream
1 tin bull's eggs
1 pint of gravy

1 loaf of breadcrumbs
2 lb. banana skins

When they set off to the supermarket follow them, but don't let them see you. When they get there and open out the shopping list, watch what happens. If they're smart, they'll turn around and come straight back. If they're not so smart they'll start looking for the items on the list!

It's a great practical joke — but a risky one. If your victim doesn't find the joke that funny, you might never see your £1 again!

63 WHAT'S UP?

In secret take a piece of paper and write the word **WHAT** on it. Fold the piece of paper and put it in your pocket. Now you are ready to fool a friend.

> **YOU:** I know what you're going to say next.

> **VICTIM:** What?

Produce the piece of paper from your pocket and show it to him.

> **YOU:** You see, I did know what you were going to say!

YOU: There were five very simple monkeys sitting on the branch of a tree. Their names were:

DOH

RE

ME

FAH

and

SOH

DOH and **RE** and **FAH** and **SOH**
fell off the tree.
Who was left?

VICTIM: ME.

YOU: So you're a simple monkey!

YOU'RE WET!

This is a joke that needs preparation.

Find a plastic bottle that has a plastic top to it that fits tightly. Make about ten tiny holes in the bottom with a pin. Now fill the bottle with water right up to the brim and the moment it's full put on the cap. Dry the bottle carefully.

While the cap is tightly on the bottle, none of the water should come through the holes in the bottom.

Now find your victim and tell him you're having a terrible time opening this bottle of water and could he help you. Give him the bottle.

The moment he takes off the cap the water will begin to pour through the tiny holes and he'll get wet!

Dress up as a ghost — but don't tell anyone what you're up to.

For a good ghost costume you only need an old white sheet, with a couple of holes for eyes so that you can see where you're going.

Dressed in your ghost suit go around haunting people. If you do it on 31st October (Hallowe'en) nobody will be surprised — so you won't be able to frighten anybody because they'll be expecting to see ghosts then. Do it on 1st January or 5th May or 19th July or September 17th and you will **surprise** people.

YOU: What is high and white and cold and has a summit and ears?

VICTIM: I don't know.

YOU: A mountain, of course.

VICTIM: But where are the ears on a mountain?

YOU: You never heard of mountaineers?

For this joke you need a PAVEMENT
VERY STRONG GLUE and a COIN — a 1p,
and a COIN—a 1p, a 2p, a
5p or even a
10p coin will do.

Cover one side of the coin with glue and
then stick it to the pavement!

Find a good hiding place, where you can
see the coin but where no one can see you, and
wait and watch. One by one the passers-by
will each bend over and do their best to pick
up the coin! They'll all fail — and feel fairly
foolish!

(If you do this trick with a 50p coin
you'll feel foolish too. Because after
you've had your fun, the laugh's on you.
You won't be able to pick up your coin
either!)

69 PYJAMA TOPS

You need a needle and thread for this joke.
You need to know how to sew too — though
not very well.

All you do is take
everybody's pyjama
trousers and sew up
the legs.

You'll only need a few stitches — and
don't sew them too tight, or the victims
will see what's happened before they try
to put on the pyjamas — and the fun is to
watch them hopping about the bedroom
with their feet all caught up in the sewn
up pyjamas.

71 WHAT A CORKER!

Put a penny piece inside an empty wine bottle and then put a cork in the top.

Now challenge a friend to get the coin out of the bottle **WITHOUT** breaking the bottle and **WITHOUT** pulling the cork out.

Your victim will think about it, then he'll give up and say it can't be done.

Well, you've fooled him. You **can** get the coin out of the bottle, without breaking the bottle and without pulling out the cork — very easily, in fact.

All you have to do, is push the cork **INTO** the bottle!

YOU: **MUM,** why did you drop that £5 note at the bottom of the rubbish bin?

MUM TURNS THE RUBBISH BIN UPSIDE DOWN IN THE MIDDLE OF THE KITCHEN AND BEGINS SCRABBLING ABOUT ON THE FLOOR FRANTICALLY LOOKING FOR THE £5 NOTE.

TEN MINUTES LATER.

YOU: April Fool!

FOR THIS TRICK TO WORK, YOU MUST CHOOSE A VICTIM WHO IS WEARING A TIE.

YOU: What does a boat do when it gets into a harbour?

VICTIM: Drops anchor.

YOU: No.

VICTIM: Sounds its horn.

YOU: No.

VICTIM: Turns off the engines.

YOU: No.

VICTIM: What does it do then?

YOU: Ties up!

AND AS YOU SAY 'TIES UP!' YOU FLICK YOUR VICTIM'S TIE UP OVER HIS HEAD!

YOU: I bet you I can clasp your hands together in such a way that you won't be able to get out of this room without unclasping them.

VICTIM: I don't believe you.

YOU: Watch.

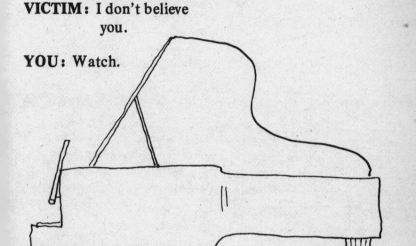

Now all you have to do is find a really heavy piece of furniture with legs — a grand piano, a big dining room table, a dressing table, a TV set on a stand — and clasp your victim's hands around one of the legs. They won't be able to escape then!

75 BLESS YOU, FATHER

At five to nine on a Sunday morning, suddenly tell everyone that you're awfully sorry but you've only just remembered that the vicar's wife telephoned yesterday to say that she and the vicar would be calling at nine that morning to find out why you hadn't been to church for so long !

Watch what happens.

(And watch out for what happens when nine o'clock comes but the vicar doesn't.)

YOU: What is green and goes boing boing?

VICTIM: A green boing boing?

YOU: Quite right. Well done. What is black and goes boing boing?

VICTIM: A black boing boing.

YOU: What is yellow and goes boing boing?

VICTIM: A yellow boing boing.

YOU: What is white and goes boing boing?

VICTIM: A white boing boing.

YOU: What is red and goes boing boing?

VICTIM: A red boing boing.

YOU: What is pink and goes boing boing?

VICTIM: A pink boing boing.

YOU: No, no, no, stupid! They don't make them that colour. Don't you know **anything?!**

77 STRONG ARM

You can prove to your friends that you are as strong as all of them put together!

Face a wall and put your hands flat against it, like this:

Make sure your arms are straight.

Now ask **any** number of people — three, thirteen, thirty-three — to line up behind you. Get each person to hold his arms straight out in front of him and to rest his hands on the shoulders of the person in front.

When everyone is in position, you shout **'PUSH!'** and they must all push as hard as they can. Try as they may, they won't succeed in flattening you against the wall — so long as you are strong enough to hold off the one person behind you. Provided you can resist the one person behind you, it doesn't matter how many other people are in the line. Each one of them is taking the strain and absorbing the effort of the person behind him.

If your mother sometimes says you don't wash your face and neck and ears properly, here's a lovely practical joke to play on her.

One night take the green leaves from the top of a carrot to bed with you.

Keep the leaves under the pillow and wake up in the morning before anyone comes into your room. Put the green leaves in each ear so that they look as if they are sprouting out of your earholes. Now lie back on the pillow and pretend to be asleep.

After a while, your mother will come into your bedroom to find out why you're not up yet. Pretend to be asleep and wait for her to **SCREEEEEEEEEEEAM** when she sees the greenery growing out of your ears.

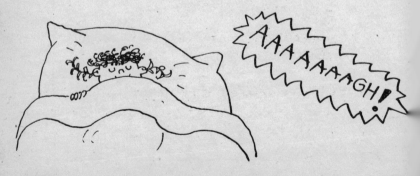

YOU: What's the difference between a **SENTENCE**, a **PUSSY-CAT** and a **POT OF GLUE?**

VICTIM: I don't know.

YOU: It's a tough one. I'll help you with a hint. A sentence has a pause at the end of its clause. A pussy-cat has claws at the end of its paws.

VICTIM: And what about the pot of glue?

YOU: Ah, that's where you get stuck!

You'll have to save up to try out this joke because you need a £1 note before you start. Once you've got your £1 all you need is a length of cotton and a tiny scrap of sticky tape. Attach the cotton to one side of the £1 note.

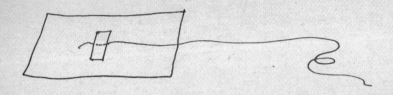

(Do it carefully because you'll want to take the tape and the cotton off the note when you've finished with the joke.)

Now find a good corner out of doors and put the £1 note on the ground on one side of the corner and hide around the other side of the corner holding the other end of the length of cotton.

When someone comes along and bends down to pick up the £1 note pull it away at once. The money will jump — and so will your victim.

81 AAAGH!

**YOU COME HOBBLING IN TO
YOUR MOTHER.**

> **YOU:** Aaagh! I'm in agony! I'm in such
> pain! I've hurt my foot! It's killing me!
> Aagh! It's going to fall off!

**YOUR MOTHER THEN LOOKS AT
YOUR FOOT. EVERY TIME SHE
TOUCHES IT YOU CRY OUT IN
PAIN! EVENTUALLY SHE BAN-
DAGES IT UP AND GIVES YOU A
BAR OF CHOCOLATE AND 50p TO
CHEER YOU UP.**

> **YOU:** You're a marvellous nurse,
> Mum. Thanks.

And you get up and walk away as though
nothing had happened. Nothing had!

YOU: Will you help me?

VICTIM: Yes.

YOU: First fold your arms.
Now put them by your side.
Now fold them again.
Now bow towards me.
Now kneel down.
Now get up.
Now shake your head.
Now close your eyes.
Now open your eyes.
Now open your mouth.
Now close your mouth.
Now clap your hands.
SLAVE!!!

Stand exactly like this, with just the tips of your forefingers touching:

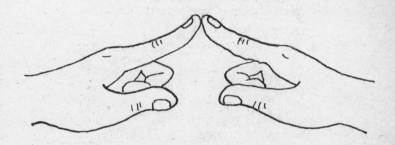

Now bet anyone anything they like that they are not strong enough to grasp you by the wrists and pull your fingers apart.

If they hold you by the wrists, however strong they are, they won't be able to do it.

YOU: Aaaagggh! There's a giant spider on the floor over there! Aaaaaaaagggggghhhhh!!!

EVERYONE ELSE JUMPS ON TO THE TABLE, SHOUTING 'WHERE?' 'HELP!' AND 'SHRIEEEEEEEEE EEEEEEEEEEEEEEE EEEEEEEEEEEK!'

TWO MINUTES LATER.

YOU: APRIL FOOL!

85

YOU: Take any number.
　　　　Now add twelve.
　　　　Now subtract four.
　　　　Now divide the number by two.
　　　　Now add three and a half.
　　　　Now close your eyes.

(The victim closes his eyes.)

YOU: Dark, isn't it?

This is a great trick that fools — and astounds — the victim every time you try it.

Ask someone to take a key from you. As you hand it to them, the key suddenly **DISAPPEARS!**

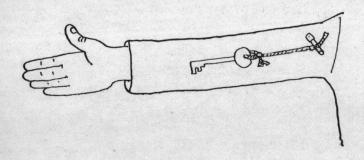

How do you do it? Well, the key is tied to a piece of elastic that goes up your sleeve. The other end of the elastic is pinned up your sleeve. You stretch the elastic when you hold the key in your hand and cover the elastic itself with your fingers. Just as your victim stretches out his hand to take the key, you let go of it and it shoots up your sleeve and out of sight!

Here's how to have fun first thing in the day. Get up very early and get completely dressed. Then climb back into bed and pretend to be asleep. Stay in bed until people start to wonder where you are and why you haven't come down for breakfast. When your mother comes in, keep your eyes shut. Wait for her to wake you. Open your eyes blearily.

YOU: What time is it, Mum?

MUM: Time you were up. You've got to leave for school in five minutes.

YOU: Don't worry, Mum. I can get dressed in ten seconds.

MUM: Don't be silly.

YOU: It's the truth, Mum. I bet you fifty pence I can get up and get dressed in less than ten seconds. Go and stand outside the door and I'll do it.

YOUR MUM LEAVES THE ROOM. TEN SECONDS LATER YOU JOIN HER, FULLY DRESSED, AND ASK FOR YOUR BREAKFAST — AND 50p!

YOU: Did you get wet before school this morning?

VICTIM: No.

YOU: I didn't think so. You can always tell when someone hasn't washed.

Here's a challenge that should fool all your friends. Take a large, heavy, hardback book and stand it upright near the edge of a table.

Now invite your friends to knock the book over **using only their breath.**

They'll huff and they'll puff, but however hard they blow, they won't knock the book down.

When they've given up you can show them how it's done. Underneath the book you have placed a large paper or plastic bag. You now blow into the bag and as it gets bigger and bigger it will topple the book over!

On the night of 31st March/1st April tiptoe right through the whole house collecting everybody's underwear. Take all the bits of underwear you can find — in bedrooms, in bathrooms, in airing cupboards — and hide them neatly and carefully somewhere in your own bedroom.

On the morning of 1st April just watch what happens.

YOU: I bet I can jump higher than a house.

VICTIM: I bet you can't.

YOU: I bet you £100 I can.

VICTIM: I bet you £100 you can't!

YOU: I'll have my £100 now please. **A HOUSE CAN'T JUMP!**

92 FANGS A LOT

Make yourself an amazing set of false teeth with orange peel.

If you cut the orange into quarters, the peel from one quarter will be enough to make you a handsome set of orange fangs. Cut them out carefully with a knife, like this:

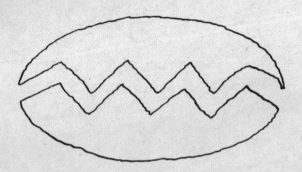

Wedge one set under your top lip and the other under your bottom lip. Don't tell anyone about your new teeth and go about as usual, keeping your mouth closed. When you're ready to make your joke — and when everyone will least expect it — open your mouth and watch what happens!

93 BEAUTIFUL SOUP!

Offer to make some soup.

Go into the kitchen and open a tin of soup.

Spend some time in the kitchen, whistling while you work.

After about ten minutes tell everyone the soup's ready and that they can come in and sit down and have it.

When everyone is sitting at the table, serve the soup. Pour it from the saucepan into each bowl very carefully. Carry each bowl over to the table blowing on the soup as you go. Say, 'Be careful now. It's terribly hot. I don't want you to burn your lips.'

Now just watch while everybody picks up their spoons and very carefully takes their first sip of the soup — only to find it's stone cold! You didn't heat it up at all!!!

YOU: I bet you I can make
you say **BLACK.**

VICTIM: I bet you can't.

YOU: I bet you £100
I can.

VICTIM: Okay. Try me.

YOU: What colours are on
the French flag?

VICTIM: Red, white and blue

YOU: There! I told you I'd
make you say **BLUE.**

VICTIM: No, you said I'd say **BLACK.**

YOU: You just did!

Collect together at least a dozen small pieces of metal and keep them in a tin mug. You can use **KEYS** and **TIN WHISTLES** and **PENCIL SHARPENERS** and **PIECES OF TIN** — anything that's metallic, fairly light, and doesn't have a sharp edge.

Now all you have to do is drop your tin mug full of metal bits and pieces on to a hard floor — and wait for your mother to come rushing into the room screaming:

'WHAT HAVE YOU BROKEN NOW?!'

YOU: I want to tell you a story, but I need you to help me to tell it properly. Each time I stop I want you to say 'Just like me'. Okay?

VICTIM: Okay.

YOU: Once upon a time, I left my house.

VICTIM: Just like me.

YOU: I walked down the garden path.

VICTIM: Just like me.

YOU: And right across town.

VICTIM: Just like me.

YOU: At the end of the town I found a wood.

VICTIM: Just like me.

YOU: I went into the wood.

VICTIM : Just like me.

YOU: I walked through the wood.

VICTIM: Just like me.

YOU: I looked up into
a tree.

VICTIM: Just like me.

YOU: And I saw a monkey.

VICTIM: Just like me.

YOU: Yes, **just** like you!

YOU: Will you remember me in fifty years?

VICTIM: Yes.

YOU: Will you remember me in twenty-five years?

VICTIM: Yes.

YOU: Will you remember me in fifteen years?

VICTIM: Yes.

YOU: Will you remember me in ten years?

VICTIM: Yes.

YOU: Will you remember me in five years?

VICTIM: Yes.

YOU: Will you remember me next year?

VICTIM: Yes.

YOU: Will you remember me next month?

VICTIM: Yes.

YOU: Will you remember me next week?

VICTIM: Yes.

YOU: Will you remember me tomorrow?

VICTIM: Yes.

YOU: Will you remember me in another hour?

VICTIM: Yes.

YOU: Will you remember me in another minute?

VICTIM: Yes.

YOU: Will you remember me in another second?

VICTIM: Yes.

YOU: Knock, knock.

VICTIM: Who's there?

YOU: So you've forgotten me already!

INKY

Take a piece of blotting paper and cut
into a few shapes like this:

Now spill a little black ink on to each
piece of blotting paper so that the ink
covers the whole of each piece.

Put the blotting paper somewhere
warm so that the ink dries.

You have now made your own ink
blots. Have fun dropping them around
the house!

This looks like a real accident — but it isn't. It looks that bit more convincing because as well as the ink blot, there's an empty ink bottle lying beside it!

Sit on the floor exactly like this, with your right hand on top of your head and the fingers spread out as wide as it is possible for them to go:

Now bet anyone anything they like that if they take hold of your forearm just above your elbow, however strong they are they won't be able to lift your hand off your head.

They'll **TRY** and **TRY** and **TRY** — but they'll fail. You've fooled them yet again.

This classic April Fool has been popular for hundreds and perhaps thousands of years. It may be old, but it still works every time.

When you're out shopping in a busy street, suddenly stop and look up at the sky. Point at it. If possible, get a friend to look up at the sky with you. Get him to point too.

Before you know what's happened, everyone will be stopping in the street and looking up at the sky! Yes, you can fool all of the people all of the time.

TEE-HEE

Looking for page 129, eh?

FOOLED YA!